D0629410

Halfway to 1984

About the author:

A member of the Diplomatic Service since 1924, Lord Gladwyn helped to draft the United Nations Charter and was Acting Secretary-General of the United Nations in 1946. He later served as Permanent Representative of the United Kingdom to the United Nations, and as British Ambassador to France. At present he is President of the Atlantic Treaty Association, Chairman of "Britain in Europe", a member of the Parliamentary Assemblies of the Council of Europe and Western European Union, and Liberal spokesman on Foreign Affairs in the House of Lords, and a Director of Messrs. S. G. Warburg & Company, Ltd.

Halfway to 1984

by GLADWYN JEBB, LORD GLADWYN

COLUMBIA UNIVERSITY PRESS

NEW YORK & LONDON

This book is based on lectures delivered under the auspices of the School of International Affairs at Columbia University in the fall of 1965

Lord Gladwyn, as Sir Gladwyn Jebb, helped to draft the United Nations Charter and was Acting Secretary-General of the United Nations in 1946. He later served as Permanent Representative of the United Kingdom to the United Nations, and as British Ambassador to France. At present he is President of the Atlantic Treaty Association, Chairman of "Britain in Europe," Member of the Parliamentary Assemblies of the Council of Europe and the Western European Union, President of the Campaign for a European Political Community, Liberal spokesman on Foreign Affairs and Defence in the House of Lords, and a Director of Messrs. S. G. Warburg & Company, Limited.

First printing 1966
Second printing 1967

Library of Congress Catalog Card Number: 66-27476
Printed in the United States of America

FOREWORD

In this book, based on lectures originally presented by Lord Gladwyn under the auspices of the School of International Affairs of Columbia University, the author has set for himself a bold task. He has attempted to paint in broad and related strokes the centers, conflicts, and mutual responsiveness of power since World War II. As a statesman playing a vital role in many of the major security arrangements and developments of this period, he writes with the advantage of a participant; yet the scope of the analysis necessarily brings into play the writer's role as an acute observer. Whether as participant or observer, Lord Gladwyn has presented an enlightening and provocative account of the major developments of the era. Writing with great candor, he leaves his readers to agree with or to dissent from the clear-cut interpretations he places on the events of the period and the roles of the men who helped to shape them. His candor is combined with courage when he extends the story to the probable shape of things in 1984, a date made famous by George Orwell.

The book, as were the lectures, is divided into three chapters on the past, the present, and the future. The first period of this forty-year span was marked by a strenuous effort on the part of the West, championed particularly by Franklin Roosevelt, to achieve Great Power solidarity both in the settlement of German questions and in the establishment of the United Nations. By 1946, the differences between East and West had become so deep and insoluble as to color the main political events and primary security considerations from that date to this. The Cold War destroyed the capacity of the Great Powers to act unitedly, whether inside or outside the United Nations, in the maintenance of peace and security. As a consequence, many new problems were created by the divisions and disagreements. In the United Nations the middle-sized and small powers in part filled the gap, and contributed effectively to the snuffing out of brush-fire wars. It was an era of bipolar power, the two superpowers confronting each other with massive nuclear strength.

The "Balance of Terror," or nuclear stalemate, represented a threat so unthinkable as to redouble efforts to avoid a major conflict.

Lord Gladwyn also describes North-South relationships and emphasizes the need for the development of a common trade and commodity policy by industrialized countries, including the Soviet Union, in relation to the great number of newly emerging nations. He assesses the character of the Western interest in the new nations and warns against the assumption that the new nations may be expected to develop national and political structures similar to our own as a requirement of their solidarity with us. Generally unacquainted with democratic forms, these countries may be expected for a long period of time to develop political institutions and practices of a special character arising out of their own experience. What really matters is that in the field of foreign affairs they maintain genuine independence and friendly trading ties with the West.

In defense of his analysis of the future, Lord Gladwyn states that "Western man cannot escape from his past any more than he can from his destiny. We must speculate or die. That is our nature." While he sees special developments in constellations of power, particularly on a regional basis, he predicts that the two superpowers will continue to hold their relative status in the scheme of power. There will be more evidences of multipolarity, marked particularly by the nuclear advances of such countries as China and France; yet, failing international agreement on nuclear arms, the balance of terror will still serve as the restraining force.

In the final chapter, Lord Gladwyn turns to other great problems confronting us: automation, industrialization, population growth, food production. He believes that food production and distribution can outrace population growth, but confesses concern about the capacity of industry to produce an ever-increasing leisure class. This trend toward an ever-enlarged leisure class is an essential challenge to "the aims of society and the purposefulness of life."

Lord Gladwyn's view of the future, inclined toward optimism, is an antidote to the thinking of those who regard the great domestic and international tensions, problems, and complexities confronting the world as defying peaceful solution.

ANDREW W. CORDIER
Dean, School of International Affairs

CONTENTS

Halfway to 1984

One

THE STRUGGLE FOR POWER SINCE WORLD WAR II

In these lectures I want to examine what has, very broadly speaking, happened to the world during the last twenty years: to see where we are now, to draw conclusions from our present state, and to peer into the future. I do not think this is a useless exercise. If history is bunk, then the future is bunk too. But somehow we do not feel that it is. In point of fact Western man cannot escape from his past any more than he can from his destiny. We must speculate or die. That is our nature.

Anyone can draw any conclusion from history, which—as Lenin shrewdly said—always turns out to be more cunning than one supposes. No computer can predict the future. There are too many imponderables. But the general drift can often be guessed by the unaided human brain. For what we have been largely determines what we are and shall be. Equally, awareness of a desired end determines, whether we are conscious of it or not, what we do now. However much the general mystique may have been shattered, the communists in China and elsewhere think they know where they are going. Whatever school of thought they belong to they must believe that the capitalists, or "imperialists," are bound to attack them. They believe also that they will come through. We think that the communists will inevitably try to overturn our society by insidious means but that we shall come through (in the sense that ultimately our values will prevail, as to some small extent they may be said to be asserting themselves now in the Soviet Union). But, except in China, such notions as these are probably less intense now than they were ten years ago. The politicians, who are usually not philosophers or historians, live from hand to mouth, being principally occupied with the essential task of maintaining themselves in power. But even they must profess some general concept. So must we all have some, perhaps unconscious, belief in ourselves and in our future. How far is this justified? How far is it rational? Are there any sure landmarks of which we can take hold? Is there any one general line which we in the West could most profitably adopt? Are we perhaps too apprehensive of the future?

Eric Blair was at school with me, though he was a few years younger than I. I got to know him only slightly in the late thirties—through my friend Richard Rees, who wrote an excellent book about him. He had changed his name to George Orwell, by which he is now universally known. His experiences in the Spanish Civil War (where he unwittingly joined a Trotskyist outfit and was very nearly executed) and subsequently in the wartime B.B.C., together with the course of world events from 1945 to 1947, all combined to inspire the celebrated prophetic work which he called 1984, published shortly before his untimely death in 1949. We are now about eighteen years away from the point when this work was conceived, and equally about eighteen years away from its *terminus ad quem*. So I will briefly recall what Orwell imagined might be the international situation in 1984.

In Orwell's 1984 three great political blocs are in existence. One, called "Oceania," consists of North America plus Britain and the old "White Commonwealth"; that is, Canada, Australasia and South Africa, and (presumably) South America. The second is "Eurasia," which extends from the Atlantic coastline of western Europe right away to Vladivostok. The third, "Eastasia," embraces China and Japan and perhaps some part of Southeast Asia as well. All these groups are governed by identical regimes of power-conscious bureaucrats, or technocrats, or whatever you like to call them, who have to maintain themselves in power by consciously restricting the standard of living, by indulging in colossal and entirely useless expenditure on armaments, by encouraging intense nationalism and xenophobia, and by maintaining permanent hostilities with one or more of the other blocs. These alliances are often changed at a moment's notice, in which case all the history books are changed and the adversary is redefined. The wars are technically about which of the groups is to control the "uncommitted" areas—notably in India, the Middle East, and Africa south of the Sahara; but in practice the chief object of the exercise is to maintain the control of the small governing groups—the so-called Inner Parties—over their own areas. Nuclear weapons are therefore not employed, by mutual agreement, and apart from a few conventional bombs dropped on the capitals to maintain "tension," such fighting as there is takes place in the uncommitted areas. We can disregard Orwell's sociological predictions for the time being; no doubt these were colored by his own unhappy experiences at school and later. But it must surely be admitted that from the purely international point of view we have already come quite a long way toward realizing his predictions.

If indeed Britain, but not Western Europe as a whole, joins some real "Atlantic Community"; if General de Gaulle succeeds in his plan to establish a "Europe from the Atlantic to the Urals" (though how could it be only to the Urals?); and if there is a real tussle in the Far East between the Soviet Union and an emergent China—all of which are real possibilities—it will be obvious that, structurally, the system Orwell contemplated for 1984 is already to a large extent in existence. Whether it will contain the more nightmarish features of the novelist's imagination is something which we cannot now foretell. But that there might be a continuing and pointless struggle for world domination conducted by other than suicidal nuclear means is also well within the limits of the possible, and even of the probable. If we do not like this prospect, is there anything we can do to avoid it? What credible counter-thesis do we favor? What sort of order would we really like, within the limits of the possible, to see established only eighteen years from now?

Before trying to answer these questions, I should like to deal in a very broad way with the international situation as it has developed since 1945 and try to see whether there were any obvious mistakes which the West need not have made, so that we can at least be warned what to guard against at the present time or in the future.

What, therefore, was our general state of mind in the summer of 1945, when the war in Europe came to an end and we all assembled at the great conference of Potsdam? Undoubtedly the scene was dominated by a desire to work with the Russians and to establish as soon as possible some world authority which would rest on close cooperation between the United States, the Soviet Union, Britain with her "Commonwealth and Empire," China, and "when she recovered her greatness" (as the rather odd phrase had it) also France. This may have been foolish, in the light of hindsight, or indeed in the light of the facts then known about the philosophy of communism; but it responded to deep feelings in the people of the West which no government at that time could possibly have ignored. The San Francisco Conference had of course just ended in agreement on these general principles —though the basic Great Power thesis of the Dumbarton Oaks Conference of the previous year was tempered to some extent by the efforts of the smaller powers to give more importance to the General Assembly than had been contemplated, while the so-called Yalta voting formula had tempered the original suggestion of the Russians that all decisions of the Security Council, apart from purely procedural questions, should be taken with the unanimous consent of the five permanent members. But the general climate was "Great Power"—as I know very well, since I was present at all three of these gatherings and together with those redoubtable experts Dr. Leo Pasvolsky and Sir Charles Webster helped to draft the United Nations Charter.

It is true that the extreme Great Power thesis was Roosevelt's own and that Winston Churchill never found it very attractive. Churchill seemed to prefer the conception of the "three overlapping circles"—the Commonwealth, the Anglo-American "special relationship," and finally Europe. He always thought more in terms of regionalism and of constructing a Council of Europe, which even then he regarded as a continental arrangement to which Britain herself would not actually belong but in which, in some unspecified way, she would participate. It was true also that Britain had never really admitted the great importance which President Roosevelt attached to

China, even though we agreed that she could hardly be omitted from the ranks of Great Powers, if there really was to be a Great Power system. It was true likewise that President Roosevelt always seemed to have his tongue in his cheek when he talked about the British Commonwealth and Empire. He certainly did his best to encourage independence movements in those parts of the Commonwealth which were at that time not completely independent. It was evident at Yalta that he was out to establish if he could a sort of dyarchy with Stalin and, behind the scenes as it were, to run the world with him. This seemed to be borne out by the extraordinary price, including the Kuril Islands and the base at Port Arthur, which he was prepared to pay the Russians—largely at the expense of China—in return for their coming into a war which was already largely won.

So there were great though unformulated reserves on the "Great Power" theory among the Western victors. But the fact remained that we had accepted this thesis, that there was no obvious counter-thesis which could be maintained if any world organization was going to be established, and that we all had agreed that there must be some kind of world organization. The difference was that, whereas Roosevelt really believed that a general agreement with Russia was not only desirable but also possible, Churchill had at an early stage and certainly after Yalta very serious suspicions that it was not. Whether the President would have voluntarily reversed his view is anybody's guess. No doubt if he had lived he would have been forced to do so. At the beginning of 1945, however, he was a dying man, and his shadow lay heavily over the conferences of San Francisco and Potsdam, before the much more realistic Harry Truman began to find his formidable feet.

It was during this period in any case that the West largely lost the peace and for the following simple reason: In 1943 the British Post-Hostilities Planning Subcommittee of the Chiefs of Staff were instructed to prepare a plan for the possible occupation of Germany. We had to make certain assumptions. One of them, I remember very well, was that there was absolutely no guarantee that Germany might not succumb to the Russians before she was "knocked out" by a cross-Channel blow—the success of which could by no means be guaranteed. It therefore seemed desirable to work out a plan whereby Germany would be divided into three zones equal from the point of view of population; for if by any ill chance we ourselves never got any further than, say, the Rhine we would at least have strong legal arguments for pushing back the Russians from the west toward the east of Germany. In any case there obviously would have been no hope of getting Allied agreement on any other formula. If, however, the Russians were going to have an equal zone in the East, it was clear that Berlin itself would then be in the Russian zone and that the only way to preserve it as the capital of Germany would be to arrange for its occupation by the three victors and for its communication with the West by means of autobahns and special air corridors. No doubt more attention should have been paid to the actual details of these communications, but it must be remembered that the policy of both our governments at that time was to cooperate confidently with the Russians, and nobody imagined that things would deteriorate so fast as to result soon in a breakup of the tripartite control of a centrally administered Reich. This plan when it emerged was, I believe, discussed with the Americans and subsequently submitted to the European Advisory Commission, which adopted it, the Russians seeming to be quite pleased—as I suppose was natural in the circumstances. The document certainly went also to Number Ten for approval, and my impression is that it was approved, though it may be that Churchill, who was heavily engaged at the time, did not immediately grasp its full significance.

In February 1945, however, there had taken place the Yalta Conference—much maligned, though I believe unjustly so insofar as European arrangements were concerned. One of the products of this conference was the "Declaration on Liberated Europe," which I had a hand in drafting along with Harry Hopkins and Secretary of State Byrnes. This excellent document, which the Russians succeeded in watering down, but not beyond a certain point, clearly established that all Allied governments, when occupying enemy territory, should make provision for democratic governments, including members of the refugee governments in London, which would be based on free elections organized without any undue delay. There were also specific agreements to the same general effect as regards Poland. The Western powers had already agreed to the establishment of the eastern frontier of that country more or less on the Curzon Line, which broadly represented the ethnic frontier; but, as Churchill said, it did not mean that because Poland had lost her frontier she should also lose her freedom. Within a fortnight the Russians had violated this agreement in respect of Rumania. Within a month it was obvious that they were violating their engagements also in respect of Poland. During the months that followed Yalta and just before the meeting of the United Nations in San Francisco at the end of April, things reached such a pitch that Vyacheslav Molotov threatened not to come to San Francisco. Eventually he did come, but the Western powers never got any real satisfaction as regards a free Polish regime, and representatives of the free Polish government that was based in London were at one stage actually thrown into jail. The situation was therefore totally unsatisfactory when the Potsdam Conference met in June; and it did not look as if the behavior of the Russians in the other occupied Eastern European countries was going to be much better.

Nevertheless, when the war ended, the Allies had advanced well beyond their allotted zones. If General Eisenhower had not been mesmerized by the desirability of allocating troops to deal with a nonexistent Nazi "redoubt" in southern Germany, there is little doubt that he could have been in Berlin before the Russians, and certainly in Prague. As it was, American and British troops ended up not far from Berlin and held Mecklenburg, Thuringia, the bulk of Saxony, and a part of Bohemia. If they had simply stayed where they were, therefore, at least four-fifths of Germany would have remained in the hands of the Western allies at the end of hostilities. Moreover, the excuse for staying where we were was evidently at hand, since the Russians had torn up the Declaration on Liberated Europe and completely repudiated their clear obligations toward the unfortunate Poles. There was, therefore, absolutely no inherent reason why we should not have torn up the agreement on the zones of occupation. Tragically, this was not to be, however. In spite of Churchill's protestations, Truman decreed the withdrawal of the Allied armies. In July Leipzig, Weimar, and Magdeburg were all handed over to the tender mercies of the Russians, and the Allied Kommandantur was established in Berlin. It is quite true that if we had forced a showdown the Russians would probably not have allowed the Allied troops to come into Berlin at all. Maybe there would not have been a Potsdam Conference either. But in the circumstances, that need not have worried us unduly. We held nearly all the trumps.

There we were, however, endeavoring to play a trusting Great Power game with the Russians, who for their part were waiting only for the total evacuation of

American troops from Germany to take over the whole of the German Reich and thus eventually to dominate the entire world situation. This period, characterized by intense friction but also by a strong desire on the part of the West to cooperate, I would call *Period I;* it lasted for under two years. Churchill fired a warning shot in his Fulton speech of March 1946, but the first General Assembly of the United Nations in London passed off well enough, and encouraging progress was made on the peace treaties with the former enemy powers (other than Germany) in Europe—these were all duly signed in December. Byrnes, in his speech at Stuttgart in September 1946, had shown, it is true, that the Americans were not going to stand any nonsense as regards Germany and were proposing to set up some kind of German administration on their own if they could not get the Russians to agree to join with them and the British in a treaty ensuring the disarmament of Germany under the supervision of a joint council of the Allied powers. But it was only after repeated failures by subsequent meetings of ministers to arrive at any such agreement, that in 1947 the real challenge was laid down with the Truman Doctrine, which involved a take-over by America of the British defense obligations in the Middle East and to some extent in Europe as well. This was followed by the establishment of Marshall Plan aid and by the historic rejection of this great offer by the Soviet Union in July. Thus 1947, which closed with total disagreement with the Russians on the future of Germany, may be said to be the year during which the whole Rooseveltian conception, including the splendid plan for the internationalization of nuclear power put forward by Bernard Baruch in the middle of 1946, collapsed; when the Russian veto in the United Nations became more and more familiar; and when the United Kingdom began the process of "disimperialization," first in India and then in Africa, which was virtually completed in the extraordinarily short time of fourteen years. The chief feature of this brief period of 1945–47 was the sincere attempt made by the West, even at the cost of some of its vital interests, to cooperate with the Russians. When it became absolutely clear that Stalin did not distinguish between the Nazis and the Western allies—both after all being, as he saw it, capitalists and imperialists—the attempt was perforce abandoned, and the celebrated "Cold War" began.

I remember coming back on the *Queen Mary* from the meeting of the United Nations General

Assembly in New York at the end of 1947. There was also on board a mysterious little man who seemed to have considerable influence in the Soviet delegation. Much to my surprise, given our pretty frosty relations with the Soviet government at that time, he asked to come and see me. Over a drink and after many circumlocutions, he confided to me that just after hostilities had come to an end there had been many people in Moscow who had wanted to get on better terms with the Western powers and who were very much opposed to the policy of Stalin. These liberally inclined persons might even, he said, have taken over power in 1946 but for one terrible event, Churchill's Fulton speech in March of that year! It may have been that there was a "liberal" party in Moscow in 1945, but the idea that they were frustrated by the Fulton speech is nonsense. You need only to read this celebrated document to see how moderate and how obviously true it was. If there had been any "liberals" in the Kremlin they should have welcomed it with open arms!

This new period—*Period II*—may perhaps be said to have lasted from 1947 to the middle of 1956. Its beginning, as I have already said, was marked by the Truman Plan and the Marshall Plan, the rejection of which by the Soviet Union for herself and her satellites was one of the most fortunate of Soviet mistakes. The challenge itself was however not really taken up by the Soviet Union until the following year, and then it became evident that they were going to frustrate the American initiative if they possibly could. On February 23, 1948, occurred the historic "coup de Prague," when the unfortunate democratic government of Eduard Benes was overthrown by the Czech Communist Party organized under the unseen leadership of Valerian Zorin, the agent of the Soviet Union. The shock produced by this move resulted in the immediate conclusion of the Treaty of Brussels, setting up what was then known as "Western Union," a defensive alliance of Britain, France, and the Low Countries. It was evident that this alliance alone could not possibly defend the West, and if this were to be done by conventional means, America too would have to deploy her full power in Europe. The United States was not yet ready for this, however—though in April of that year Foreign Minister Bevin sent me to Washington to explore the possibility of some wider defensive arrangement, and negotiations in the Pentagon with representatives of the U.S. State Department and the Canadian government led to a tentative draft treaty which was very similar to the treaty actually signed a year later. But only the blockade of Berlin which started in June of that year persuaded Congress that the joint defense of Western Europe was absolutely essential to the interests of the United States and of all the other Western allies. Before NATO was set up there were few American troops in West Germany and not many British either. Had it not been for the nuclear bombers which the British government permitted the Americans to send over to British bases, the whole continent probably would have been overrun; or at the least, procommunist governments would have been installed in many Western European countries.

The Russians did not press the challenge to the point of war. In May 1949 the Berlin Blockade was lifted, shortly before the NATO Treaty was signed. One might have thought that the Cold War crisis had been finally resolved by resolute Western action. Not so. Only a year later, just after the Communists had taken over the mainland of China, the North Koreans invaded South Korea—the beginning of a fierce conventional war of three years' duration, which resulted in a virtual draw. It seems probable that the North Korean action—which undoubtedly was encouraged by the Russians though probably not by the Chinese —was the result of a genuine misreading of remarks made by Dean Acheson and Senator Tom Connally, conveying to the uninitiated the impression that Korea was outside the defense perimeter of the United States. Whatever the reason, World War III seemed quite clearly to be on the horizon, and the rearmament of the Germans was a logical result.

All through this period one of the main features was confident Anglo-American cooperation, which reached its highest point perhaps when the Commonwealth Division successfully operated in Korea. It was also the great period of NATO and saw the establishment of rather less successful copies of NATO in the Middle East and in Southeast Asia. The containment of aggressive communism everywhere was the slogan and in the circumstances a perfectly justified one, since there was then such a thing as World Communism and it did work in accordance with a common strategic plan. Finally, though the United Nations was to some extent paralyzed politically from the outset by the Russian refusal to cooperate, there is no doubt that in the period 1947-56 the world organization had some notable achievements to its credit: There was Palestine, where United Nations intervention did after all result in the end of hostilities; there was Korea; and for that matter, there was the clearing-up action after Suez. It is true that one of these achievements was due in part to the fortuitous absence of the Russians and to the conferring of additional power on the General Assembly by the resolution of December 1950 entitled "Uniting for Peace," which some members still consider to be illegal. But until the end of this period the Western powers, under Anglo-American leadership, had a "built-in" majority in the General Assembly and consequently the Russians were not really able to exploit the United Nations for Cold War purposes. In Dag Hammarskjöld, elected Secretary-General in 1953, the United Nations discovered an administrator of genius, who helped a great deal to give some political content to the struggling organization. But I repeat that all this comparative success really rested on United States predominance and Anglo-American cooperation.

Even the death of Stalin in March 1953 did not really disturb this general picture of a confrontation of the "Anglo-Saxons" and the Soviet Union. Georgi Malenkov probably wanted to reverse Stalin's policy altogether and arrive at some genuine arrangement with the Western powers, but he had not the power to do so—though Lavrenty Beria, had he been successful in his attempted coup d'état, might have tried. (Beria was supposed not to have favored the suppression of the Berlin uprising of June 1953.) Even under the joint regime of Marshal Bulganin and Nikita Khrushchev various initiatives took place in 1954. The most notable of these were the Austrian State Treaty, the reconciliation with Yugoslavia, and the famous but quite ineffective "summit" meeting at Geneva in October 1955, which merely confirmed that the Russians were simply sticking to Stalin's policy with regard to Germany. But these were no doubt in the nature of holding operations. The real change took place in February 1956 when Khrushchev denounced Stalin in the remarkable speech before the Twentieth Party Congress of the Communist Party of the Soviet Union. This resulted in the triumph of Tito; the "destalinization"—and effective partial liberalization—of most of Eastern Europe, accompanied by a virtual uprising in Poland; the collapse (after a rather desperate struggle in the Central Committee in January) of the so-called dogmatists and the departure of the seemingly indestructible Monsieur Molotov after nearly twenty years of devoted service. It also resulted in the suppression of the Hungarian Revolt which, from the

Soviet point of view had really gone too far. But the "liberal" ground lost here was gradually recovered later. Obviously a new era was beginning.

As I see it then, *Period III*, so far as world politics are concerned, started in 1956—and went on until the end of 1964. It may be described as the period extending from the pulling down of Stalin's statues to the explosion of the first Chinese nuclear bomb. Indeed, more specifically, the whole period coincides with the rise and fall of that genial Russian peasant, Nikita Khrushchev. Toward the end of 1956 also the great Russian nuclear program was beginning to bear fruit. Though it seems that the first Russian intercontinental ballistic missile was not successfully tested until the summer of 1957, the Russians undoubtedly knew that they had a powerful new and perhaps decisive arm when they indulged in their own threats of nuclear retaliation at a moment when the Anglo-French Suez expedition was evidently not going to succeed. Stalin indeed had "bequeathed" the hydrogen bomb to Russia, but this could not really much improve the strategic position of Russia unless she had also the means of conveying it to a target. Once she had that—and for a time she seemed to have a definite lead over America—the period of the Cold

War "confrontation" was ended and that of the nuclear stalemate, or "Balance of Terror," had begun.

One of the effects of the achievement of the Balance of Terror in 1957 was the gradual loosening of the alliance systems on both sides of the Iron Curtain. (The Suez crisis at the end of 1956 had no doubt started the process in the West, but that event can now be regarded as a kind of exasperated aberration in an otherwise steady course of "disimperialization.") There is no great reason to be surprised at or alarmed by this inevitable development. During the Stalin period it had been strategically essential for each side to accept the physical leadership of its most powerful member. But as soon as the point was reached (or seemed shortly to be reached) when both giants could knock each other out, even on what was called a "second strike," it was obvious not only that the secondary allies were less essential but also, paradoxically, that they had much more freedom of action. Certainly none of the secondary allies could act against the wishes of both giants—Suez proved that, if nothing else—but they could, if they wanted to, do things which might not be very pleasing to their own senior partner. Another essential feature of this period was the fact that since the Russians were now less frightened of the "imperialist" attack predicted by their holy books, they were at liberty to try to extract concessions from the West by maneuvring and negotiation and to pursue the rather aggressive policy which, ironically, came to be known as "peaceful coexistence."

This was essentially Khrushchev's line. He was—indeed he still is—an extremely clever man, who in many ways resembles the late Ernest Bevin. He thought that with the new power of the Soviet Union behind him—the first Sputnik appeared in October 1957—he could successfully bully, blackmail, or somehow negotiate his way toward a Berlin settlement which would eventually place West Germany at his mercy and thus produce by other means the result consistently aimed at by Russian policy since the war. At first he had the full support of China, and 1958 was taken up at first in demands for a summit meeting (largely provoked by the Middle East crisis). But it was at this stage that the first cracks in the Sino-Soviet common front appeared. Khrushchev backed up the Chinese to a certain extent in their offshore islands demonstration, but it became increasingly clear that he was not going to go further than that. His eye was always on Berlin—and on America. Toward the end of the year the challenge came. Either the Western powers must agree to Berlin's becoming a demilitarized free city, or the Soviet government would sign a treaty with the D.D.R. (the East German administration) and all dealings on Berlin would thereafter have to be conducted with that government—and it was quite clear what that meant.

The challenge was fended off. Khrushchev thought that when Prime Minister Macmillan arrived in Moscow in February 1959 wearing his white fur hat it was a gesture of surrender. He discovered that he was dealing with a man as clever as he was; though it is true that Macmillan did come rather near to agreeing to things that some of the Western allies considered, perhaps with reason, to be dangerous. A meeting of foreign ministers followed in Geneva. Still no progress. Then Khrushchev played his long meditated card: he would go to Washington himself to "work" on General Eisenhower. He also proposed to sell himself to the great American public. In both directions he had some success. In particular he always alleged that at Camp David the President came close to admitting his central thesis about a free city of Berlin. When it gradually became apparent that this was not so, his fury knew no bounds. He thought that at a summit conference he might nevertheless extract a few concessions. Why exactly he wrecked it nobody may ever know. It is thought that the remnants of the Moscow dogmatists—who had always been pretty suspicious of his efforts—persuaded him to do so just before he left for Paris, using the V–2 incident as an excuse. Thereafter he waited for Kennedy, thinking the Democrats would be more forthcoming. The 1961 meeting in Vienna proved the reverse. He resolved to achieve his ends by other means and to approach Berlin via Cuba. We all know the result. President Kennedy's historic stand in November 1962 saved the Free World. Khrushchev lingered on for another two years but perhaps he himself no longer knew what he was doing. Soviet relations with China got worse and worse and eventually ended, as it were, with a bang. The world had reached another turning. How Khrushchev managed to keep himself in power for two years after Cuba is a mystery. But eventually his enemies closed in. His fall more or less coincided with the first Chinese nuclear explosion and the perpetuation of the Sino-Soviet rift. Since then Russian policy has been virtually nonexistent, and it is evident to all that we are in a new period.

The unwritten rule of the Balance of Terror is that

neither side is at liberty to go beyond a certain point without courting instant destruction on a colossal scale. Why Khrushchev ignored this simple but major principle may never be known. Perhaps even his closest colleagues did not know. After Cuba, however, one thing was entirely clear, namely that war between the two existing giants had become virtually impossible. The corollary of this was that the so-called territorial status quo wherever their forces were in contact was likely to be maintained until such time as one, or the other, or both came to the conclusion that it was in their material interests to change it. It is here that we may perhaps also detect the second great feature of this period, to which I think I have already alluded—namely, the increase in the freedom of action, if not in the ultimate importance of the secondary allies on both sides of the Iron Curtain.

On the Western side the period opened with the signature of the Treaty of Rome in March 1957. It now seemed that Western European union, which had broken down badly with French rejection of the European Defense Community in 1954 and had been maintained in only a small way by the successful conclusion of the Coal and Steel Community in 1952 was an increasing possibility. With the coming into power of General de Gaulle in 1958, France—partly as a member of the Common Market and partly through her individual efforts—became more and more dissatisfied with what she believed to be American hegemony; and though it is quite possible to maintain that the nationalistic ambitions of present-day France are not compatible with the achievement of a United Europe, it is evident that neither European nationalism nor European union is compatible with a Western Alliance, or indeed with an Atlantic Community, which is based on absolute American predominance.

Had the effort of Britain to enter the European Economic Community not failed as a result of French opposition, it was probable that this circle would have been squared and that a United Western Europe would have been by now a happy partner in a reformed Western Alliance. It is perhaps still probable. But at the moment all we can say is that fissiparous tendencies have weakened the Western Alliance and that this process has undoubtedly been assisted by the so-called Balance of Terror. Equally, on the other side of the Iron Curtain, the complete inability of the Russians to prevent smaller allies from asserting their interests both in economics and in foreign policy has been marked. Poland and Rumania, at any rate, now seem to be almost as recalcitrant in the East as France is in the West. Since nuclear war appears to be impossible, they see no particular reason why they should not profit from the maintenance of the status quo between East and West. It remains to be seen whether, in the East or in the West, the idea of a grand alliance can be maintained at all in the circumstances.

Finally, a major feature of this crucial period was the Sino-Soviet rift. It started with an ideological quarrel; it comprised the withdrawal in 1960 of all Russian technical aid to China, which is supposed to have retarded Chinese industrial development by about ten years; but it nevertheless ended with the explosion of a Chinese nuclear device. In principle, the rise of this great country with its almost unconcealed designs on East Siberia, Mongolia, parts of Soviet Central Asia, and America's new ally, Japan, to say nothing of certain districts of India and Burma, should result in the two existing nuclear giants' coming closer together, or at any rate less far apart. For obviously it would be difficult or even impossible to contain China if she could rely absolutely on either of the two present superpowers. Unfortunately the tendency toward some understanding between superpowers was frustrated at the end of our period by the war in Vietnam. However much the Soviet Union may wish to do so, she can hardly dissociate herself altogether from North Vietnam; it is therefore evident that some kind of solution for the Vietnamese problem simply must be found which will enable the two superpowers not to get in each other's way anywhere in Asia. Yet another tendency which could be observed during this period was the increasing difficulty of reconciling a reduction in tension between Washington and Moscow with any effort to incorporate West Germany on an equal footing in the Atlantic Alliance. Many people alleged that this problem was insoluble until such time as West Germany, and eventually all Germany, might be peacefully integrated in some Western European community which, in its turn, might be in some kind of special relationship with the United States and yet on good terms with the Soviet Union.

During Period III the United Nations, too, largely changed its character. From having been a chiefly Western-oriented affair it quickly developed into a machine largely dominated by the "emergent" nations. This phenomenon produced one qualified success in the Congo—thanks largely to the inspired leadership of Dag Hammarskjöld—but otherwise resulted in much frustration. It became apparent that the resolution "Uniting for Peace" was not ideally suited as a basis for "peace-keeping," and that the ultimate choice in this respect was between political futility and Great Power, or at any rate superpower, unanimity. It also became apparent that, short of a world state and a common world philosophy, no world authority could function except on the basis of a reconciliation of major group interests. The smaller powers, therefore, could assert their points of view successfully only if they actually formed part of some larger grouping.

These, then, were the main features of what I have called the first part of our progress toward 1984. Before we consider the present world situation, are there any lessons which we—the present members of the Western Alliance—can profitably draw from the strange tale that I have been narrating?

The first lesson we can surely draw is that for the West not to give anything to the Soviet government except for something concrete in return is a policy which pays handsome dividends. It was not carried out in July 1945 when we pulled back our troops in Germany, with obviously disastrous results, but it was applied in the first, Stalinite, Soviet pressure campaign on Berlin and again during the rather different Khrushchevite campaign, which had the same general objective. Both these were examples of collective resistance on the part of the Allies. There was also the splendid individual example of the exercise of United States will when the attempt was made to turn their flank by placing missiles in Cuba.

The second lesson may be that the Allies were wise not to use force to support the East Berlin revolt against the Communist masters in 1953, to come to the rescue of the Hungarians in 1956, or to knock down the Berlin Wall with tanks when it was first constructed in August 1961; for all such actions could hardly have failed to result in fighting. Once fighting starts there is absolutely no knowing where it will end. Besides, as we have already noted, the Soviet yoke in the satellite countries is now becoming generally less and less severe. If in the absence of any direct pressure by the Western powers the Soviet satellites are nevertheless becoming increasingly independent, why risk a world war to foster the process? We may, therefore, so far as Eastern Europe is concerned, and even so far as the prospect of the ultimate reunification of Germany is concerned, profitably put much of our faith in the simple healing force of time. There is some faint prospect now of coming to terms with the Soviet Union, but if we had tried to force the issue earlier, there would now be no such prospect.

The third lesson is that as long as the Balance of Terror endures—and it will probably endure for a considerable time—there is no need to be unduly alarmed by an apparent loosening of the Western Alliance, nor should the Russians be unduly alarmed by such phenomena either. For unless one nation, whether in the East or in the West, is prepared to take the plunge and actually join the other side—which seems to be inconceivable at the present time—the alliances on both sides of the Iron Curtain will in practice rest on the ultimate power of the nuclear deterrent at the disposal of each of the superpowers. Subject to this, it is clear that anything which encourages a greater unity from both the economic and the political points of view is desirable, if only because very small and totally independent units are not viable in our modern age. The tendency of the Europeans, including the British, to unite should therefore still be encouraged, this being the surest way to prevent the Alliance from becoming too loose altogether and to prepare for the Atlantic Community of tomorrow.

The final lesson would seem to be that the abandonment by industrialized Western powers of their right to "protect" their own interests in all parts of the world does not appear to cause these interests to suffer much material damage. The Suez Canal, which the British and the French were so desperately keen to deny to Nasser, is now seen to be a perfectly free waterway, and British trade with the abandoned Indian subcontinent is greater than it ever was. Nowhere is France more popular than in her ex-colonies. Holland is at present, it seems, the most popular Western country in Indonesia. We are now assured by all concerned that whatever else may be the reason, it is not to protect British interests that we have some remaining bases in the Indian Ocean. It would seem to follow logically that you are really better off if you make no effort to enforce your will or even to protect your ex-protégés from some fate worse than death, and that even America might improve her position if she withdrew militarily from certain outlying areas in Asia; that is to say, when she can do so without losing face, abandoning her friends, or giving her adversaries any notable advantage. But more about this in the next chapter, where I attempt to analyze the present world political situation. All I would add here in regard to the extraordinary and unforeseen happenings since World War II is that everything might well have been very much worse. We can, at least in the West, survey the situation with a certain satisfaction and say, with D. H. Lawrence, "Look, we have come through."

Two

THE PRESENT NUCLEAR STALEMATE, OR BALANCE OF TERROR

The distance we have already covered in the short time since Orwell meditated his remarkable prophecy is almost incredible. As we saw in the last chapter, the whole face of the world has changed since 1947. Empires have vanished, new empires are emerging, societies are collapsing, man may be about to set foot on the moon. At the same time the technical possibilities of reducing the earth to something like the state of the moon, or (more optimistically) of Mars, are increasing yearly. The pessimists who maintain that man has attempted to assume the functions of God and is therefore bound to destroy himself may yet be justified. H. G. Wells once wrote a book called *Mind at the End of Its Tether.* He was wrong, of course. There was indeed a world war, but humanity survived, and large sectors of it are now much better off in every way than they were then. Thus we should not in any way despair. After all, Orwell predicted a nuclear war in the fifties (he wrote his work before the hydrogen bomb had prepared the way for the Balance of Terror), and that, at least, we have avoided and indeed seem likely to avoid. The greatest dangers are perhaps those which seem to be inherent in all industrialized societies, whether controlled or free; but we will come to that in the next chapter. Let us now see where we are, internationally speaking, at the present time—in this curious period in which it might be said that we are "between two worlds: one dead, the other powerless to be born."

The main feature of the present landscape is the so-called Balance of Terror, or nuclear stalemate: the capacity of the United States and the Soviet Union, if not to "knock each other clean out," at any rate to inflict quite unacceptable damage on the other even on a "second strike." This situation clearly involves acceptance by both sides of the territorial status quo in all areas where the two sides are in physical contact and in a good many where they are not. So far as can be seen, this situation can be changed only by the successful development on either or both sides of an antimissile missile. The experts tell us that this is highly improbable, since staggering costs would be involved in achieving such immunity, or near immunity, from attack by a superpower. It may be possible, however, to devise a system which could give a superpower relative immunity from attack by a minor nuclear power, though not, of course, vice versa. If this is so, then a certain amount of nuclear proliferation—the possession of a small, or very small, nuclear potential by a number of secondary powers—though highly undesirable, may not be such a great danger as is commonly thought. For apart from anything else, there is a fairly strong possibility that were a secondary power to threaten the use of, much less use, nuclear weapons, *both* superpowers would move against it, if necessary in combined action. If a third power became a superpower in its own right, this would of course no longer apply; but how near are we really to the day when there will be a third superpower? I myself believe we are a long way off, for the following reasons.

The only new superpowers—that is to say, powers of the same magnitude as the Soviet Union and the United States—which might conceivably emerge before the end of the century (to say nothing of 1984) are a United Europe and China. But a United Europe has not been formed yet, and may indeed never be formed in a nuclear sense at any rate. Moreover, its achievement would presumably depend on active German cooperation, and that could produce an explosive situation which the Germans themselves would no doubt be the first to wish to avoid. China, for her part, probably will be able to produce the equivalents of Polaris submarines and long-range Minutemen missiles in considerable quantities only when she has become fully industrialized; and few suppose that will be before 1984, at the earliest. She might have a few medium-range ballistic missiles mounted in silos, or even on submarines, before then, but nothing equal to the second-strike capacity of the United States or the Soviet Union. If this is true for China it is even more true for India. Unless quite surprising progress is made in achieving a politically united Europe, and unless (which seems quite impossible if Britain joins) such a European union decides to go ahead with a major nuclear program, in accordance with "third force" ideas, nuclear "tripolarity," "quadripolarity," or (as is sometimes even feared) "multipolarity" will not, I suggest, come to be in our lifetime. The great nuclear giants are thus likely to remain the United States and the Soviet Union; and the achievement of a limited nuclear status by a few other powers in addition to Britain and France (who might conceivably combine their efforts one day) should not vitiate the logical political consequences of the present Balance of Terror, at any rate not for a long while. It seems quite possible, moreover, that the possession of a limited nuclear capacity may make nations more rather than less cautious in their handling of potentially explosive situations. In particular, the Chinese seem to be much more cautious now than they were in 1950, during the Korean War.

All this is subject to one major qualification: Should Japan, the first victim of nuclear warfare, ever seriously turn her energies to constructing nuclear armaments then we could certainly expect a third "nuclear pole"—and a pretty unstable one—to appear very rapidly, especially if Japan worked in cooperation with the Chinese. But such a development seems quite unlikely. It is true that in a few years China will be capable, in theory, of inflicting great damage on Japan, but presumably only at the expense of being blotted out herself by American nuclear power. It is true also that China can exert strong historical and economic pulls on Japan; and if the Chinese play their cards cleverly, or the American theirs not so cleverly, this may be a great factor in future world politics. But as things are now it does not look as if such a development would be rapid or likely soon to affect that nuclear bipolarity which I believe is going to endure, short of a third world war.

Nevertheless, under the cover of this great umbrella with two handles many things seem now to be happening. In the first place, as we have already noted, both the Atlantic Alliance and its Communist equivalent, the Warsaw Treaty Organization, are in difficulties. Owing to the Balance of Terror many argue that war between what used to be called the East and the West is now out of the question. Why, therefore, spend vast sums on conventional armaments which will clearly never be used? In particular, if you are a small- or medium-size country having difficulty with balance of payments, why go out of your way to contribute more than a bare minimum to the common military cause? We all know the answer: The adversary must not be tempted to make small incursions in the hope of gaining limited political objectives, confident that he can get away with it unless nuclear power is employed, and confident also that the other side will not employ nuclear power, except in the event of general hostilities. Even so, the sense of danger—"the ties of common funk," as it used to be called—has certainly deserted the Western Alliance to a considerable extent. CENTO never had it very much; and though SEATO should, and perhaps to a certain extent does, have it, the organization is little more than a planning body at the moment, for the general political situation in Southeast Asia is even more complicated than the situation in the Middle East.

What, then, are the principal features of the present political situation, the great facts which now loom before us? There are perhaps four: first, the gradual rise of China and the possibility (though by no means the certainty) that she may extend her influence over all Southeast Asia; second, the present crisis in the unification of Western Europe; third, the revolutionary implications of the tendency of the "underdeveloped" nations to become poorer and the "developed" to become richer (a tendency which is finding expression currently in Africa in the attack on White domination south of the Zambezi River); and, fourth, the apparent, perhaps temporary, withdrawal of the Soviet Union from any very active role in world politics—a strange reversal of the ebullient attitude maintained through the 1956–64, Khrushchev period.

In China all efforts will apparently be devoted toward building up heavy industry; but in spite of the recent success in exploding a nuclear device, it probably will be many, many years before Chinese heavy industry will be on a par with the industry of the Soviet Union or the United States. There is no doubt that in these circumstances, China will seek to increase and expand her power by endeavoring to install pro-Chinese revolutionary governments wherever possible in the underdeveloped countries. If she were successful in installing such governments in Southeast Asia, then she might be able to build up some kind of economic and commercial system which would assist her own development and partially solve the question of her food supply as well. Any further success she might have in Africa or South America would be designed simply to weaken the presumptive power of America rather than to increase her own. What does not seem at all likely at the moment is that the Chinese would seek to pour in armies or even officials into the countries whose governments had become Communist and in principle pro-Chinese, if only for the fact that this would give rise to frightful resistance problems, however nominally Communist and pro-Chinese the regimes in theory were. Tibet may be cited in contradiction; but apart from the fact that the Chinese have always claimed that Tibet was essentially within the actual boundaries of China, this is a very underpopulated country, the centers of which can be fairly easily controlled, though even here considerable resistance is still being encountered in the mountains. Nor is it certain even that the Chinese would be physically capable of occupying the various countries of Southeast Asia, especially if it were not possible for them to reinforce their armies by sea. Even less, with their exposed communications over the Himalayas, would it be possible for the Chinese successfully to invade, occupy, and administer parts of India. Such nightmares should really be discounted from the start. The Chinese might conceivably lop off pieces in outlying areas of Ladakh or Assam and in regions in the north of Burma, but even that is improbable at the present time.

Broadly speaking, one may say that, just as the Russians have now realized that in the last resort they cannot risk a war with America, so the Chinese may come to the same conclusion, after years of perhaps not very successful efforts to exert their influence in the underdeveloped countries. One thing is certain at any rate: The Chinese armies could not advance very far outside China in one direction or another without running a considerable risk of general, and hence of nuclear, war, for which they are not at the moment and will not for many years be prepared. Nevertheless, it may well be that some states, particularly in Southeast Asia, are likely to have some kind of "special relationship" with the Chinese; and in certain circumstances it might not be intolerable if this were to occur. There are now great and active Chinese colonies in Malaysia, Indonesia, Borneo, and elsewhere, but these colonies are not necessarily bound to be the nucleus of some overseas Chinese Communist Empire.

We approach the second main feature of the present world situation as I see it; namely, the present uncertainty—not to say crisis—in the gradual formation of a Western European community. The emergence of a supranational body in Western Europe, which seemed very probable until June 30, 1965, when General de Gaulle effectively withdrew his delegation from Brussels, is now by no means certain. If any member is entitled to say that, rather than agree to something which it does not like and which the other partners do like, it will withdraw its representation and have no further part in the proceedings, then it is difficult to see how the community can work, except on the basis of the hegemony of one particular power. Though the community could in theory continue almost indefinitely as a simple customs union—if that were all that the parties could agree to—there is no possibility of going beyond that and forming an economic, still less a political, union of any kind, unless there is some element of "supranationality." As I have said, the only way in which a non-supranational entity, whether economic or political, can possibly be run is on the basis of the hegemony of one power, in this case France; and it is quite unlikely that the other powers will agree to such a hegemony. Even less likely—supposing Britain were a member—would be the establishment of some kind of joint, Anglo-French hegemony (theoretically arguable, perhaps, if a distinction is made between the two nuclear European powers and the others); for there is no reason to suppose that the Germans would agree to a secondary status for themselves. Consequently, if Britain were a member, a supranational solution would be the only practicable one. Thus, whether Western Europe can now continue on its way toward becoming a political entity is in the lap of the gods, and we cannot confidently predict the issue.

But another obvious feature of the present situation is that there is no real chance of forming any valid or enduring Western European community unless Britain does join and one or two members of the present EFTA join also. For if Britain and certain other European states do not join, then the probability seems to be that the British Isles will tend to gravitate closer to the United States, in accordance with the scheme recently put forward by Senator Javits, while the largely uncoordinated states of the mainland will try and no doubt fail to make some deal with the Soviet Union about the future of Germany, after which some of them also may wish to join the Atlantic Customs Union. There is a great deal to be said in favor of the Atlantic Customs Union idea; but in the first place, it will obviously take some time to be established and, in the second place, we must try to think exactly what it might represent in political terms. Clearly, if it were formed at all, it would contemplate something more extensive—in other words, some eventual political union. Otherwise there would be little point in it. (All customs unions inevitably pose this essential question.) If political unification were set on foot and prospered, the countries of Western Europe—apart from those sections which might prefer to come within the Soviet orbit—would inevitably become part and parcel of America politically; that is, they would have common political institutions. And it is difficult to see where these common institutions could be based except in the United States. This would mean, in other words, the acceptance by Europeans of an American political system. Such a situation might give rise to real difficulties, for the American "Americans" would be outnumbered about two to one by the European "Americans"; thus, if the system were entirely representative and democratic in accordance with the majority views of the U.S. Constitution, the American "Americans" would no longer be in control, and even the present Constitution of the United States might be liable to considerable changes. If the Customs Union did not develop to this extreme point, on the other hand, it could work only if the nominally independent European powers included in it were in fact the equivalents of American satellites and had no really autonomous foreign policy. Of course it might be that only the British Isles and perhaps one or two of the Scandinavian states would join the Union and that the remainder of Western Europe would constitute itself as a separate entity; but this separate entity could be built up only by the acceptance of supranational power, and that seems quite unlikely.

Nevertheless, it still appears probable that in spite

of the setback of possibly two or three years imposed by the present attitude of the French government, the European Economic Community will eventually proceed on the path to full economic and political unity, as contemplated by the authors of the Treaty of Rome, and that, when this becomes manifest, the United Kingdom and other EFTA states will either actually join this new Community or be closely associated with it. Let us hope so, because on the whole this still seems to be by far the most desirable solution for the whole Atlantic world, since it would enable us to build the Atlantic Community on the basis of the "two pillars" of President Kennedy. And it might be only under such a solution that we could arrive at a peaceful reunification of Germany. For on the alternative basis of an Atlantic Customs Union, America's political frontiers would be fixed finally on the Elbe; and it is hardly to be imagined that the Russians would not do everything in their power to prevent the further eastward extension of these boundaries. It is therefore to be hoped that the United States will continue to favor the idea of Western European unity within the framework of the Western Alliance, which means of course that, rather than push the alternative solution of some Atlantic Customs Union, she should encourage Britain to wait and join the European Community at the first opportunity. It is possible, however, that if France should effectively disrupt the EEC, to say nothing of NATO, some Atlantic Customs Union embracing Britain and perhaps also West Germany might be the only answer. But even if this came about, the existence on this side of the Iron Curtain of states outside the Western Alliance could be nothing but a disruptive force and a great temptation to the Russians to expand their influence westward by what would obviously be represented in the circumstances as "peaceful penetration."

This is the sort of situation which may well arise if the concept of the totally independent nation-state prevails in Western Europe and no concessions are made to the tendency of our present industrial system to divide the world up for purposes of markets into larger and larger economic blocs. But if such blocs are formed, how far can the underdeveloped, or developing, countries escape being associated with one or the other of them? This is a question which has a direct bearing on the recent sinister tendency of such countries to get poorer and poorer while the "developed" countries get richer and richer; in other words, for the terms of trade to go against the developing countries.

In spite of all efforts, chiefly by the United States, to produce "aid" for such countries, the fact that on the whole they get much less for their products than they did on the world markets usually cancels out all the benefits of the aid. At the same time, the population in most of these countries increases by leaps and bounds, which also serves to cancel out the effects of economic aid. If this state of affairs goes on, there is no need to talk about the dreadful effects of communist propaganda. Some kind of revolutionary situation, even if only chaos and anarchy, will arise by the very force of things in most of the states concerned, and the industrialized countries will in that case be largely to blame. What should be done?

Well, clearly the first objective—and at this stage it can be only an objective—is to try to coordinate all the industrialized countries (including the Soviet Union and the states usually associated with it) in a policy for both trade and aid to the underdeveloped countries. Presumably this would involve internationally agreed-on schemes for the bulk-buying of selected commodities, the establishment of long-term credits, the devotion of a fixed proportion of national incomes to non-military aid, and some means of relating aid to the terms of trade—of increasing aid proportionately if the prices of certain foodstuffs and raw materials went down on the world market. All this may well not be possible until there is a united Western Europe which can negotiate as a whole and as an equal power with the United States, Japan, and the Soviet Union. But already the Brussels Commission is supposed to be negotiating for the EEC in the "Kennedy Round" of world tariff-cutting negotiations, and if Britain and others joined the EEC this system would doubtless continue. Furthermore, the forum OECD exists now in Paris. It cannot function properly in the absence of a common political will. This will does not exist at present, partly as a result of the remains of the Cold War, and partly owing to the regrettable division of Europe and indeed of the whole Western Alliance. But that would not necessarily prevent the United States from initiating a great new project and suggesting—on the assumption that some progress can be made in the direction of Western European unity—that it be discussed in the OECD with the Soviet Union, which could be requested with its allies to join the organization.

I think that some rather spectacular initiative of this kind by the United States might have a great impact. Perhaps such a move cannot be successfully made while the Rhodesian crisis smolders on and the conflict in Vietnam continues unabated. But these crises may come to an end sooner than we think possible, and it is clear that there will be no world war over the first and probably none over the second either. In any case, the idea of a new Marshall Plan, this time not solely American and this time for the whole planet, ought to make an immense appeal; and even though it might not be realized for some time, it might well encourage desirable political tendencies, not only in Europe but in the world generally. Would the Russians play? Perhaps initially they would profess to regard it only as another "capitalist" or "imperialist" plot to weaken the "popular democracies," just as they turned down the first Marshall scheme, preferring Stalin's Cold War. But things have changed a great deal since 1947, and I must say I wonder what would happen now.

Exactly what is happening in the Soviet Union is always a mystery, but there is no doubt that we are now far from the roaring, rampaging, "We-will-bury-you" mood of Khrushchev; for the Russians are now recognizing that they cannot challenge the United States, and it is obvious that they have already lost the leadership in "world revolution" to their enormous neighbor. At the same time they are immensely strong, at least in defense, and have also the capacity, if they wish, to build up a strong, dynamic economy by encouraging increased production of consumer goods and changing some of their basic conceptions about the "wickedness" of a market. I have the impression that this great people—which still controls something like one-sixth of the surface of the globe—is now seriously brooding over its future, and that it will eventually decide to be, not something essentially alien to the bulk of the world, but an ordinary superpower (if one may so describe it), equivalent to those now existing or which seem likely to be formed in the future. There is a great deal of evidence that the Russians, particularly the younger Russians, are getting bored with Communist doctrine, especially with the messianic role which their governments have for so long adopted, and that as a people they are longing for really peaceful coexistence, in place of the bogus type of coexistence which has been so far insisted on by the authorities. There is no doubt to my mind that the creation of a Western European Union including Britain which would not rule out the long-term prospect of some withdrawal of American troops from Europe to America would strongly assist such a development in the Soviet Union. That is, of course, provided Western Europe remains in the Western Alliance, and consequently under the ultimate protection of the American nuclear umbrella.

One of the greatest determining factors of the present situation, however, which I have not alluded to yet, and which, greatly daring, I now propose to touch on, is the present mood of the United States. What I say about this may be wrong, since I have not been in this country very much lately; I base myself on information derived from occasional conversations with Americans and from the press. But it seems to me that in the United States since November 1962 there has been, happily, a great recovery of national confidence, lately reinforced by the short lead which the Americans apparently have obtained over the Russians in the conquest of space: the great achievement of Gemini II is still echoing round the world. The Cuban missile crisis also represented a tremendous victory for this nation, one which it won quite independently of its allies, who were hardly consulted before the really big decisions were made. It seems to me also that recent decisions to take direct action in Vietnam and in Santo Domingo—again with little or no consultation with allies—are symptoms of this increasing national confidence. And if the Americans should come to the conclusion that they actually must administer South Vietnam on the lines of what was known in the bad old days as colonial rule, that would be a manifestation of complete self-confidence (though no doubt a misguided decision). I think that in principle this self-confidence is in itself a very good thing, and I suggest that the real reason for it is that the United States has now realized that if it actually wants to impose its will almost anywhere in the world, it is in a position to do so without risking nuclear war. I say "almost anywhere in the world" because in areas the defense of which the Soviet government regards as absolutely vital, such an attempt would certainly result in nuclear war. But the Soviet government obviously does not regard what is happening in Southeast Asia as affecting its vital interests; and other areas, in Africa, South America, or even certain outlying parts of Europe, might well come into this category also.

The real question therefore seems to me to be, Do the Americans want to constitute what I suppose might be described in old-fashioned terms as an "American Empire"? Or—assuming that they do not want this—are they being pushed toward it against their will by some mysterious destiny, by the inexorable logic of events? Do they, for instance—supposing that what is vaguely regarded as "Communism" seems likely to establish itself in some country in South America, Asia, or Africa—feel compelled to resist this development by physical force, even if that should mean ultimately taking over the country's government and wholly running it? If, as I believe, they do not, then they should make up their minds to come to terms occasionally with revolution. This does not mean that they must necessarily "appease" an enemy. Of course not. What is "appeasement" anyway? —about the most overworked word in the English language. Giving in to an enemy who is resolved to destroy you and who manifestly might do so unless you stand up to him, is certainly a bad thing; we have known that since the days of Danegeld. Here we can all agree. But international relations are rather more complicated. Would America be in mortal danger if a government calling itself communist took over power in some minor state in Africa, for example? (If I am not mistaken, this actually happened not so long ago in Zanzibar.) First, we must determine what sort of communism is involved. There are now many varie ties. Some might be of the Yugoslav type—but Amer ican relations with Yugoslavia are now quite good. Some might be pro-Russian, or pro-Chinese, or even Trotskyite—in other words a sort of nonaligned communist government. What would have to be weighed is not whether the revolutionary government in power was "communist"—whatever that may mean—but whether it constituted a real, physical menace to the United States, either directly or by close association with Russia or China in a way that was liable seriously to affect the present strategic balance of the world. I can think of quite a number of states—even those producing valuable raw materials such as oil, sugar, or nonferrous metals of various kinds—where it would not matter very much whether they were "communist" or not. For it probably would be very difficult for either Russia or China to absorb beyond a certain point the products of such a country, except on terms which would be highly disadvantageous, in which case the country would very likely continue to trade with the West, to avoid starvation. Certain Western firms might be nationalized of course; but if neither Russia nor China could afford to take the main products, the Western countries could always retaliate with pretty powerful results if they were not adequately compensated.

The criterion governing the use of physical force, then, should be whether the new government would be likely to side with either Russia or China in such a way that the world balance could be tilted against the West, and notably against the United States. If Russian or Chinese troops actually turned up in the country concerned, for instance, that might well constitute a *casus belli*. But I believe that this would happen only if Western Europe, or a part of it, left the Western Alliance and sided with Russia, or if Japan did the same in regard to China. Perhaps one or two countries in Latin America can be placed in this category as well. If Mexico, for instance, declared itself an ally of either Russia or China and began installing modern missiles, something would clearly have to be done, as it was done with Cuba. But in general I suggest that only Western Europe, Japan with certain outlying islands (including Formosa, for the time being), the Philippines, Australasia, and also (for the time being) South Vietnam should be regarded as within the perimeter in which America and her NATO allies actually would take physical action if political events demanded it. The remaining countries of the world would be told that what regime they had was of no concern to the West unless it adopted a frankly hostile attitude and broke off relations, in which case they could hardly expect either to receive aid or to maintain satisfactory commercial relations. But no action beyond that would be taken. In other words, the developing countries could have any regime they thought fit, including any kind of communism if they were so foolish as to prefer it. Such a declaration, I am convinced, would in no way encourage developing nations to become communist. On the contrary, I think, it would make the United States more popular than it has been for years and might materially diminish the chances of a communist take-over in the "third world."

This would not mean, of course, that in the case of proved aggression from without—notably aggression by a superpower—we would abandon our right to take forceful action, particularly if it could be done under Article 51 of the United Nations Charter; but basically we, the NATO allies, should firmly maintain that the political complexion of any country's government is in itself positively no concern of ours. If the United States subscribed to some such principle as this, it would at least dissociate itself from the image now forced on it by its enemies in the developing countries; namely, that it is reactionary, militaristic, neo-colonialist, racialist, and generally opposed to all change, even when the conditions of the ordinary people of a country are horrible in the extreme.

I shall be told, I am sure, that this is an immoral doctrine: revolutions are normally the result of force and are therefore undemocratic. This is all too true. But it is unfortunately also true that democracy, as we know it, is not understood by about four-fifths of the human race. Therefore we cannot hope that revolutions, which are necessary when things become intolerable, will always be conducted by democratic means. What we must hope is that when they occur they will not necessarily result in the establishment of tyrannies, and in particular that the resulting governments will be well disposed toward the Western powers and will not tend to see in them an inevitable enemy.

Where, then, does an examination of present tendencies lead us? What conclusions may we draw? Let us resume them as follows: Bipolarity will continue; though the existing alliances will endure they may well become looser; Western Europe may, and if possible should, still be united; China is perhaps less of a menace than has been suggested; a new effort should be made to apply Marshall Plan principles to the whole underdeveloped world, and if possible the Soviet Union should be associated with such an effort; America, having regained her confidence, should not fear revolution per se and should not seek to repress it anywhere in the world. If these principles apply, what may we think about the more remote future, about 1984? That will be the subject of the next chapter.

Three

THE SUPERPOWERS OF THE FUTURE

Supposing that I have analyzed present world tendencies in the least correctly, supposing too that we can avoid a major nuclear war, what can we then predict for 1984?—when the readers of this book will for the most part, no doubt, be distinguished professors and administrators, and I myself shall be only 84 (and I trust at least as healthy and vigorous as ex-Chancellor Adenauer).

Since predictions—saving those of inspired prophets—are usually contradicted by events, I confess it would interest me enormously to conduct an inquest in that fateful year, on why the ensuing speculations went wrong, or alternatively to observe the extent to which the human race moved in the interval in the direction that now seems indicated by its general interest. So let us now peer resolutely into the future.

The political passions of man are such that it would be insensate to suggest that the next eighteen years will be anything but a period of tremendous struggles all over the world. In Europe the danger is that the tremendous energies of a German nation intent on reunification may, unless they are directed into the peaceful construction of a new type of European Community, either spark off a world war or open the way to Russian domination of the entire continent and the constitution of Orwell's projected Eurasia. So might, in theory at any rate, any ultranationalistic activities on the part of the French. The one hope for Western Europe is that it will come together in some form of frankly supranational entity, including Britain. And I shall go right out on a limb and suggest that by 1984 such a body will have emerged, in friendly association with an Eastern Europe still in close contact with Russia, and that both sections of Europe will cooperate with the two superpowers, as well as Japan and certain South American states, in some kind of reconstituted OECD, which will no doubt still be functioning in Paris. This might be thought of as an Atlantic Community, but the conception is clearly wider than the strict Atlantic area.

There is little doubt that by 1984 China and, to a lesser extent, the Indian subcontinent will have become fairly heavily industrialized. To a lesser extent again, this will be true also of Indonesia and Southeast Asia in general. But I do not think that these great areas will cooperate with the Western world, organized on a "two pillar" basis, in the same way that Japan, or even the Soviet Union, are likely to cooperate—though no doubt there will be continuing economic and social cooperation on a world scale in the United Nations (whose survival I confidently predict, even if its Security Council and General Assembly should be greatly modified). The reason is that I do not detect any desire on the part of the Chinese or the Indians to adopt Western civilization. Their fear of domination, of a destruction of ancient values, probably will persist. The Chinese may adopt Western techniques but they will not accept Western values, although the Russians—who are after all partly Europeans—may do so. As for the Indians, or rather the Indians and the Pakistanis—but in spite of the present divisions I feel that by 1984 some kind of partnership will have been worked out between Hindus and Muslims—here again I feel that Western industrial civilization will suffer some kind of sea change before it is adapted to local conditions. Conceivably, too, as in the past, some great character—an Asoka, an Akbar, a Clive, or, if you will, a super-Nehru—may emerge who will form the modern equivalent of an

Indian Empire. I do not think this is impossible, in spite of the unifying force of modern world communications, and their theoretical tendency to suppress local characteristics.

The same sort of thing might happen even in the Middle East, where there are now several candidates for the extinct title of leader of Islam, though at the moment there is no chance at all that any one candidate will be able to achieve predominance. But the irritant of Israel, which will doubtless persist, for the Israelis have powerful friends, may one day produce a pearl in the body politic of the Arab-speaking Muslims. There is a common language and a common culture in all the Arab lands, and though the emphasis is on Arab nation-states at the moment, it is possible that such tribalism will be worn down by 1984 by the sheer pressure of modern inventions. What is sure is that the Muslim way of life will not be permanently suppressed or essentially transformed by these inventions. Ancient civilizations are never totally suppressed in such a way as this. They may enter periods when they are temporarily submerged, but they later reemerge and assert themselves, or adapt the dominant civilization to their own special needs and traditions. The probability, I believe, is that by 1984 the old Islamic world will be more united than it is now but will not form an entity as Western Europe, the ancient "Christendom," could if it decided to do so.

In Southeast Asia there is no such common culture. The Malays and the Indonesians are mostly Muslims; the Burmese, the Siamese, and the Cambodians are mostly Buddhists; the Filipinos are mostly Christians; the Vietnamese partly so; the Chinese on the other hand, are mostly "Chinese," being held together more by their nationality than by a common religion. The inhabitants of this area are also much separated by history and tradition. What is their future? It certainly looks as if the area will undergo an enduring struggle for influence between the West and China. After all, the base of the area is Australasia, which is part of Western civilization, whereas the northern part has, historically, had strong links with China and, so far at least as Burma is concerned, also with India. From the natural tendency of things, therefore, there may possibly be one day a sort of federation of all the Malays to the south and a collection of states to the north which would preserve their individual identity but would nevertheless be largely associated with an overpopulated China. And China in any case may have to rely on the surplus rice production of the region. What I do not see, frankly, is any great overspilling of the Chinese people into Southeast Asia, or huge Red armies driving all before them, or even an array of Chinese Communist bureaucrats trying to discipline the equally civilized and not very well disposed local inhabitants. Even if fear of Western nuclear attack is removed, I doubt whether we shall hear much about Chinese "aggression" in this part of the world. Where the surplus population is perhaps more likely to direct itself, if it is allowed to, is into Mongolia and northeastern Siberia, or even parts of Central Asia. And all that will be the concern chiefly of the Soviet Union.

In Africa south of the Sahara the new states emerging from the old colonial "artifacts" are likely to disappear and be replaced by tribes slowly adapting themselves to the industrial process. By 1984, too, the South African whites will no doubt have been obliged to come to terms with the Bantu, either by permitting the evolution of a mixed society or by concentrating their white population in the southern tip of the continent. But I see no great wars sweeping over Africa, no great massacres of whites by blacks or blacks by whites, no mass immigration of Indians or Chinese (save only, perhaps, by general consent, to the greatly underpopulated island of Madagascar). I see only widespread disorder which will gradually be curbed, probably by local dictators making greater and greater use of locally educated technicians.

In South America we must suppose that new regimes will have rectified extreme social injustice to some extent and that "left-wing" or "popular" governments possibly will be in command in several countries. Such regimes might still be dictatorial in essence, but if the countries concerned have really achieved the "takeoff" in the Rostovian or Mexican sense, they are likely to be milder than the governments of the late, lamented Colonel Battista and his totalitarian successor. The process of industrialization here as everywhere else, undoubtedly will compel a measure of international cooperation and unification; and in the largely non-Indian southern area this should be fairly easily accomplished. The Central American states should—and probably will—combine further; and there may be one or two other such unions. But in any case a development of OAS techniques is likely if America comes to terms with revolution (as I believe she will have to), since there will still be very strong reasons for trade with the United States. Hopefully, the new regimes in South America will quickly realize that reliance on the communist powers—themselves still undergoing the throes of industrial development —will not suffice for their essential needs and that only the West, primarily the United States, can help them forward on the path of industrial progress. You may say that this means accepting communism and trying to live with it. Perhaps, but communism is not what it was. It is not now a sort of world religion like the early Islam, determined to impose itself on the infidels and offering the simple choice of death or conversion. Many features of our free type of society are now penetrating the former citadel of Marxism-Leninism, the Soviet Union, and by 1984 there may not be much difference, morphologically, between the political structure of the Soviet Union and the United States. This does not mean that there will not be continuing ideological differences—politically, there no doubt will still be many—but it could mean that some kind of cooperation may come about in regions such as Latin America and parts of Africa and Asia.

So much for our glance at the possible political regions of 1984. Some of them obviously have more chance of being formed than others. We have seen that a United Europe—whether made up only of the present Western Europe or of Western Europe with one or two of the states now in the Eastern bloc—

probably will emerge as a superstate. If a United Europe does not emerge, however, there will of course be only three superstates in existence: "Atlantica" (the United States, the United Kingdom, and possibly one or two other European fringe states), "Eurasia" (the Soviet Union and most of Europe, for I entirely discount the possibility of superpower status devolving on only the existing European Economic Community), and China. (The formation of a United Europe is clearly preferable, but we cannot ignore the alternate possibility.) In addition to these three or four great independent, or at least autonomous, regions, can any other areas develop to the point where they might constitute separate power blocs? Of the remaining six areas which we have briefly analyzed, only Japan (if she remains independent of China), the Indian subcontinent, the Arab countries, and conceivably the region embracing the Philippines, Indonesia, and Malaysia would seem to have any prospect of achieving such a status; though some might assert that if Latin America passes successfully through a revolutionary stage, she too would be ripe for such a formation. Any black African group can almost certainly be excluded.

It is entirely possible that by 1984 we will have

reached a stage in which certain national groups that are not yet completely united politically can at least combine to elect one of their members to represent them in a newly constituted United Nations Security Council. At the same time it is not wildly optimistic to think that, if the present nuclear stalemate continues and extends also to China, the tendency of the various regions to settle their own disputes may be increased. Matters for the Security Council then would increasingly be major questions transcending the interests of the regional group as such (e.g., migration issues, disarmament, or the possibility of concerted Great Power action if some local row cannot be coped with by the machinery of the region concerned). It follows that if such a system is feasible in 1984—and why should it not be?—the role of the United Nations General Assembly will be less important. Instead there should be regional assemblies where the individual points of view of the various states concerned would find expression. A "European parliament" could be one. An "Atlantic assembly" might be another. The existing Commonwealth Parliamentary Association might be a third, for nothing could be better fitted to perform a liaison between the various regions than the Commonwealth. It is possible to imagine other similar bodies which could largely replace the present "town meeting of the world." And a reformed Security Council, constructed on the lines I have suggested could not possibly be accused of being "neo-colonialist" or under the influence of one superpower more than another. Finally, if countries such as Britain, France, and Germany were willing to forgo separate representation in a world council, why would smaller countries insist on separate representation in a world assembly, which would be quite useless if the council functioned at all efficiently and quite powerless if it did not?

You will see that what I am contemplating is really a "world authority" and in no sense a "world government." I think that we may have to wait for at least another century before anything like a world government becomes even remotely feasible. It does not seem conceivable to me that by 1984 we shall have reached the point at which a common "democratic" ideal will be accepted by the entire human race, making it possible to have either genuine proportional representation of all national states in some central governing body, or a world state which will have replaced all existing nations. For that to come about would first require that there no longer be any disparities between peoples, that all countries attain similar standards of education, consumption, production, social services, law, human rights, and so on. It would require, moreover, a generally shared conception of what the end of all human activity ought to be, a common philosophy which would permit one code of human rights and morals.

Are we then to suppose that a Balance of Terror will still dominate the scene? Perhaps so, for my "World Authority of Regions" does not imply that the members of the Security Council would be totally disarmed. But I have already said that I do not foresee any real "multipolarity" even by 1984, and the hope would be that as now between the two nuclear giants some kind of agreement will have been arrived at whereby nuclear arms are limited and even gradually reduced. It is possible that a minor nuclear war will take place between regions or within certain regions. But I do not think that such conflicts would be more than flashes in the pan, even if highly dangerous flashes. As I have said, if there were a real risk of a major nuclear explosion, one or both of the superpowers undoubtedly would act to prevent it. All that is needed is essential agreement between the superpowers with the consent (as we should hope) of a majority of the other political regions.

But will not this conception be vitiated by the "population explosion" and by the desperation engendered by mass misery and starvation in many regions? I agree that this may be so, but I am less pessimistic about it than many much more learned and qualified persons. In the first place, I believe that the population explosion has been exaggerated—not in all countries, but certainly in some. I recently read what seemed to me to be a well-informed article to the effect that Chinese statistics have been bogus for years and even now the actual population of that country may not exceed 450 million. (Africa south of the Sahara may have more inhabitants than we think; but then this district as a whole is underpopulated anyhow.) Moreover, great efforts are now being made in India and also in China, I believe, to restrict the population by modern birth-control methods, which, as I was recently assured by India's head planner, are having a considerable effect. In any case it is an observed fact that the birthrate tends naturally to decline as industrialization is accomplished; and whether we like it or not, the whole world is now in the process of being industrialized. This may be a slow process, but I suggest that by 1984 the world birthrate will be going down, not up. Of course there will be a gigantic increase in population, no matter what we now do.

That is inevitable. But when people talk about world population inevitably leading to some major catastrophe, that I doubt. More likely there would be enduring misery.

The world food supply, however, is likely to increase enormously. Already the chief problem is not to produce enough food to feed everybody in the world, but to get it into the hungry bellies. If my suggested cooperation between the industrialized powers can be worked out gradually and the Cold War ended in the next eighteen years, there is no reason why the distribution problem should not be largely solved, and famine, widely eliminated. In India, at any rate, if age-old religious practices could be done away with and the whole agricultural system reorganized, a vast increase in local food supply would be possible. I am optimistic enough to think that in this direction also considerable progress will be made by 1984. If we are optimistic we may believe that modern communications —television, radio, etc.—will gradually erode even the most obstinate and ancient prejudices.

All this seems to me possible, and even probable. There are thus many reasons to be optimistic about the future of the human race, provided that we can avoid a major nuclear war (and of course this now means any major war)—a huge proviso, but everything depends on it. Failing a quite unlikely agreement on general disarmament, one method of preventing major hositilities is the Balance of Terror, which seems likely to endure. But there is another factor which clouds the prospects for 1984: the question mark which hangs over the future of the advanced industrial societies themselves, particularly over the most technologically advanced country, the United States—though many phenomena which are observable there are observable to a lesser extent in Britain, Europe, and, oddly enough, in the Soviet Union. Their future depends on the aims of society and the purposefulness of life.

There is no doubt whatever that by 1984 cybernetics will result in a huge increase in what used to be called "the unemployed," but which will be described by then as "the leisured class." As more and more factories become "automated" (as the horrible modern jargon has it), fewer and fewer workers will be required in industry. In the distributive trades and the clerical occupations the same inevitable tendency will be at work: Why employ a man if a machine will do the job more cheaply? (Perhaps the principle should not apply in communist or socialist societies, but there is reason to suppose that it does just the same.) If those forced out of a job by machines are not paid adequate compensation—as is often the case now in many civilized nations—it can be said, as it was said of sheep in the later Middle Ages, that "machines are eating men." It does seem sometimes as if machines actually were taking over our societies. (A century ago Samuel Butler made the frightening observation that one day, instead of children, there would be jolly young machines romping about on the lawn.)

There is only one possible answer to this persistent challenge. The new "leisured class" must be heavily subsidized by the state—shall we say to the extent of $3000 per annum per ex-worker—or the goods produced by the machines will not be consumed. By 1984 this class may number about twenty million people in the United States. In Britain by that time we shall perhaps have only about two or three million people in this category. How many there will be in Europe is anybody's guess. There, no doubt, the use of surplus labor from the Mediterranean countries will be more economical than automation for a longer period of time than in Britain or the United States. But eventually if the process of industrialization is pursued to its logical end, fewer and fewer people will be required in all manufacturing and allied processes wherever the machine has been adopted, and that now means virtually everywhere in the world.

Granted, therefore, that by 1984 a large section of the population in many countries will be pensioners of the state, with no work to do, how are these people to be kept happy? What meaning is to be given to an idle existence? This is something to which our planners have certainly given insufficient attention so far. When the British Labour government began introducing the welfare state in 1945—as a result of many plans drawn up by the wartime coalition government—they very likely felt that if only a living wage could be assured to everybody in Britain and the general standard of living could be steadily increased, all would necessarily be well. But they forgot that man cannot live by bread alone, that in human societies it is passion that spins the plot, and that, as Meredith has it, we are "betrayed by what is false within." Here we must appreciate that in our modern societies "work"—that is to say, employment which has some creative element—is gradually being replaced by "labor"—employment in which there is no creative element at all. Even in the higher strata of our societies this deplorable principle seems to be exerting itself.

Art, it appears, is becoming more and more either a hobby or a private joke. Even science seems to be reducing itself to a sort of routine. Any intelligent person can pursue the lines of research laid down by the great geniuses of the past; all he needs is technical training and a computer. As for the exploration of outer space, it gets more and more boring as time goes on. The idea of sitting in an exiguous capsule for days, weeks, or months, in a state of weightlessness and with nothing whatever to do, in order to land on a desert so appalling that in comparison Dante's Inferno would be a sort of paradise, or to attain a planet on which a human being would be boiled alive, is not really a very alluring prospect when you come to consider it objectively. Can it be, therefore, that it is some dim apprehension of a pointless future that is really responsible for recent outbreaks of hooliganism, vandalism, and apparently gratuitous crime? Can it be that the basic reason for the riots in Los Angeles or Notting Hill is not racial feeling, but rather the corrosion of the only cement that can bind a free society together, the principle of loving one's neighbor as oneself? With these somber reflections let us consider what alternatives are possible for the social structure of our man-made industrial Elysia only eighteen years from now.

One alternative might be disruption, a revolt against the machine, a sort of modern Luddite movement, with bonfires of computers and mass massacres of scientists. Government would be taken over by the forces of organized crime and would be run in accordance with Mafia-like rules, on a basically low level of morality. If modern machines *were* destroyed, however, and a deliberate return were made to primitive techniques of production, it would be impossible to keep the bulk of the population alive. Thus, there must always be some government at hand with a number of armed supporters to prevent the "Luddites" from having their way. This government might still be organized crime, it is true. If so, its chief object would necessarily be to perpetrate its rule and the profits of that rule. And it would have difficulty in doing so, for any gang which has seized power could be turned out by another gang. The system would not be very dissimilar to that which prevailed in the late Roman Empire.

Another possible result of "leisure" and boredom might be a situation like that described by Orwell in 1984, though he purposely exaggerated its nightmarish qualities. One party seizes power and stays in power; although its sole object is to stay in power, it has a lunatic ideology which serves as both an excuse and a powerful weapon. The standard of living is kept low deliberately, all energies being subordinated to military objectives. Society is hierarchic, and all decisions are taken by the Inner Party—a small, self-perpetuating group—in a manner which remains a mystery; though ostensibly, it is Big Brother who rules. Nobody is certain whether Big Brother really exists, but all the resources of the mass media are devoted to proving that he is all-wise and all-knowing. The society is really held together by organized hate of another society; the grand enemy is Love.

Exaggerations apart, it cannot be denied that this kind of situation is possible. Even now, in nearly all major regions of the world, we can detect a personage who might qualify as Big Brother. We can also discern, I fear, a basic mass hysteria that could easily be exploited by an able group intent on establishing some form of totalitarian state. Conventional wars between the major regions, when and if they are politically consolidated, are also possible. One has only to observe what is happening in northwestern India today to realize that, anachronistic as conventional warfare may appear, it is only too likely to occur within a given region when there is no world authority to prevent it. But supposing that strong totalitarian parties existed, at least in the major regions, would such regimes really engage in "conventional" wars against each other (the Balance of Terror presumably ruling out nuclear wars)? I do not think we need be as pessimistic as this. It is difficult to imagine that conventional wars could be limited by mutual agreement; though it is possible to imagine that the nuclear powers might take different sides in any wars that might break out within other, less cohesive political regions. The point I am making here is that totalitarian administrations within the regions, particularly the industrialized ones, are by no means impossible in 1984. And there is no reason to suppose that such administrations would necessarily be communist; they might be right-wing just as well. Totalitarianism seems to me to be a sort of psychological disease, and I agree with Norman Mailer when he defines it as a cancer within the body of history which "reduces to the leader's formulation of jargon such emotions as awe, dread, beauty, pity, terror, calm, horror, and harmony." One of the main objects of anyone who still believes in a reasonably happy future for the human race must surely be to resist totalitarian tendencies so far as possible and to stand up for the free expression of minority opinion, no matter where or how this may be expressed.

One of the chief reasons for totalitarian tendencies is fear: fear of hunger, fear of death, fear of oppression, even fear of the unknown. These fears may be irrational and unfounded, but if unchecked they can often produce the result that is feared. It seems to me that one of the best ways to check such fears, so far as international affairs are concerned, is to achieve a genuine, workable political balance. Such a balance is clearly out of the question in our modern world so long as the pursuit of purely nationalistic ends by entirely independent nation-states creates a situation of international anarchy. We must therefore provide for increasing political unity wherever possible. It is possible now in Europe; it is possible, at one remove, in our Atlantic world; it is possible even for "Atlantica" and the Soviet Union. The more other regions are organized so as to promote unity, the better the balance will then be. This is the main reason behind my theory of major political regions and, as I said at the beginning of this chapter, even if we do not think that the development of such regions is likely by 1984, we should do everything in our power to encourage their formation in the years to come.

I recognize that I have not attempted to predict what is likely to happen to our Western world if we do manage to avoid both totalitarianism and the total collapse of society with the triumph of organized crime. This is no doubt the most difficult prophecy of all. It must here be admitted that, however outdated and dangerous nationalism is under modern conditions, it is a force that binds people together and inspires them to do great things as well as horrible ones. Besides, at the moment, it is the only driving force in international affairs. The age of empires is over; even the Russian Communist "Empire" shows signs of disintegrating. Unless the activities of nation-states are curbed by an acceptable substitute for empires nationalism will undoubtedly involve us in a new sequence of wars. And wars, at least on any large scale, must now be avoided at all costs. Therefore allegiance to something larger than a nation-state evidently must be created. And only so can a motivating, unifying force be produced which will enable us to avoid either totalitarianism or total collapse.

In spite of the present grip of pure nationalism, there is no reason to abandon the notion of broader political allegiances. Even as things are, many nations have been incorporated into larger wholes; for example, Scotland and Wales in the United Kingdom, and the Ukraine in Russia. It is true that such unions usually have been established by force, but even so the union has not essentially destroyed the personality of the nation. If future unions can be established by consent, as is the case in the still emergent European Economic Community, there is no reason to suppose that there would be any material diminution of what is called the national personality. Indeed, it is not "nations" that are responsible for our modern anarchy, but only "nation-states."

Assuming, then, that by our fateful year several such unions will have come about, there is little doubt that a general diminution of fear in the world may itself have done something to eliminate totalitarian tendencies. It remains to consider what other means there may be to curb nihilistic urges resulting from the despair of modern society and the apparent pointlessness of life. Some maintain that only a religious revival can avert an ultimate collapse of human society. But what is meant by "religion"? Totalitarianism itself is a sort of perverted religion, and that is what we chiefly want to avoid. The German prophet, Oswald Spengler—whose cyclical theory of civilization has hardly stood the test of time, but who was a provocative figure of great erudition—detected in the later stages of his civilization (which according to him, inevitably ended up in world dictatorship) what he called a "second religiosity," that is to say something akin to, but other than, the burning religious convictions which usually characterized the civilization's earlier stages. This feeling was no longer expressed in missionary zeal but tended toward mysticism, such as quietism or other strange cults, which often produced great inner satisfaction. I think that this phemonenon is observable now in the Western world but that, far from being deplorable, it is one of our safeguards against the seeming futility that leads straight to the riots, the massacres, or the gas chambers of our modern world. The strangest and most dubious religious sects are pillars of society compared to the S.S. or the Secret Police or even to potentially totalitarian legislators. Apart from such manifestations we may fairly confidently expect an increase in monasticism generally and in such religious practices as Zen Buddhism. In no circumstances should such tendencies be repressed in this age of the cybernetic revolution; on the contrary, they should be encouraged. Let the Amish finally come into their own!

Yet something more than this is required and perhaps the eventual message will be revealed to us only by the last great prophet of our age. There is no real reason why the human race, even in the last stages of the industrial process, should abandon itself to lust, mass-murder, hatred, nuclear war, and almost total extinction, letting Nature train up the ants and the grasshoppers to take our place. A sharing of what wealth there is in any given society is perfectly possible. As for what to do with our leisure time, small "courtly" circles of educated and civilized people can certainly indulge in the old delights of music, verse, acting, conversation, cooking, and making love. (One virtue of modern civilization is that time for all this is possible without the assistance of slaves.) Even those of no mental attainments at all can get great pleasure from gardening, or taking part in sports (rather than merely looking on at them or gambling on them), or hunting, or fishing, or swimming, or I know not what. At the end of his appalling adventures, Candide came to the conclusion that the only thing that really mattered was to cultivate his garden. This is still the final word of wisdom so far as reasonable people are concerned. The only trouble is that there are not very many reasonable people.

So what can we look forward to, what, more particularly, can we work for, in the next decade or two? No Utopia, no visionary world state, no world empires, no infallible guides, no disciplined collectivist societies. No self-sufficient nation-states, no space escapes, no neo-colonialism, no proselytizing communism, no mass hysteria, no triumph of organized crime. But rather the gradual emergence of regional groups of nations (or ex-nations) capable to a large extent of coping with their own affairs and the firm establishment on this basis of a World Authority of Regional Representatives, trained in political skills and having at their disposal, at least in the more advanced industrialized states, a body of able administrators concerned with the whole problem of aid and development, and fundamentally inspired by Albert Schweitzer's great dictum that "it is only giving that stimulates." If this is our collective aim there is hope for all of us.

With Matthew Arnold I say therefore: Fear not, life still leaves human effort scope. But since life teems with ill, nurse no extravagant hope. Because thou must not dream, thou need'st not then despair.